# JULIUS CAESAR

by
William Shakespeare

## Student Packet

Written by:
Maureen Kirchhoefer, M.A.
and Mary Dennis

**Contains masters for:**

| | |
|---|---|
| 3 | Prereading Activities |
| 1 | Study Guide (three pages) |
| 1 | Vocabulary Activity |
| 1 | Literary Analysis Activity |
| 1 | Creative Thinking Activity |
| 2 | Drama Activities |
| 2 | Critical Thinking Activities |
| 2 | Review Activities |
| 3 | Vocabulary Quizzes |
| 5 | Comprehension Quizzes |
| 2 | Final Exams (essay and objective) |

**PLUS**

Essay Topic Suggestions
Ideas For Projects
Detailed Answer Key

---

**Note**
Any text of *Julius Caesar* may be used with this guide as references are made by act, scene, and line number.

---

ISBN 1-56137-304-4

© 1998 Novel Units, Inc. All rights reserved. Printed in the United States of America.
Limited reproduction permission: The publisher grants permission to individual teachers who have purchased this book, or for whom it has been purchased, to reproduce the blackline masters as needed for use with their own students. Reproduction for an entire school or school district or for commercial use is prohibited.

To order, contact your local school supply store, or—

Novel Units, Inc.
P.O. Box 791610
San Antonio, TX 78279

# Prereading Activities

In addition to being a tragedy or tragic melodrama about power, friendship, betrayal, and revenge, *Julius Caesar* is a political history about the Roman Republic that existed long before the birth of Christ. It's important that students understand some factual information about Julius Caesar and the Roman form of government. As you provide the information below, students can complete the Fact Sheet. The Fact Sheet may also be used as a research activity. For a Cooperative Research Activity on Shakespeare's background, see the Teacher Guide for *Julius Caesar.*

### Activity #1: *Getting the Facts: The Roman Republic*
The Roman Republic existed as early as 510 B.C., but it did not gain supremacy until 190 B.C. The form of government of the Roman Republic is the basis for many modern governments. Roman government comprised two chief magistrates or *consuls* who were elected annually, a large group of lesser magistrates, the Senate, and the popular assemblies. Power lay first in the hands of the wealthy *patrician* class, but *plebeians*, or common people, were eventually extended the right to hold state office and other rights of citizenship.

Bribery, greed, and corruption, however, were the real rulers of Rome. As the republic defeated country after country, the generals and Senators shared the plunder. The countries were required to pay tribute to Rome as well, and this money went into the hands of the patricians. Even the commoners who held office were easily swayed in their votes by payoffs coming from the wealthy. Many small landowners sold out, unable to resist the excellent offers made by the patricians. But the prices of everything had skyrocketed, and the small farmers were soon out of money. They went to Rome to join the ranks of the unemployed.

The conflict between the aristocrats and the common people grew, and several ambitious army commanders entered the political scene in Rome. Julius Caesar was one of these. In 60 B.C., the first triumvirate was formed by Pompey, Crassus, and Julius Caesar. When Crassus died, conflict between Pompey and Caesar brought the country to civil war. Caesar defeated Pompey in 48 B.C. and the remainder of his armies by 45 B.C. He returned to Rome a popular hero and enjoyed a very short-lived dictatorship. He was assassinated by republicans who feared he would turn the republic into a monarchy with himself as king.

Marcus Brutus, one of the assassins, had supported Pompey during the civil war but had been pardoned by Caesar afterwards. Caius Cassius was an outstanding general in Pompey's army, and had also been pardoned by Caesar. He initiated the conspiracy to murder Caesar.

It is interesting to note that although Caesar was born into a patrician family, he allied himself with the popular party through his first marriage to Cornelia. When she died, he married Pompeia, but divorced her in 62 B.C. and married Calpurnia three years later. Although he had no children by any of these marriages, it is suggested that his lover, Cleopatra, had a son by him, Ptolemy Caesar.

The "real" Caesar is famous for the line, *"Veni, vidi, vici,"* which means "I came, I saw, I conquered." Shakespeare's Caesar is perhaps even more famous for the lines *"Et tu, Brute?"* ("You, too, Brutus?") and "Cowards die many times before their deaths; The valiant never taste of death but once."

After Caesar's death in 44 B.C., Mark Antony and Caesar's grand-nephew Octavius joined Lepidus in the second triumvirate which pledged to avenge Caesar's assassination. They swept away their senatorial opposition by having most of the senators murdered. The armies of Brutus and Cassius fought the armies of Mark Antony and Octavius Caesar. Brutus and Cassius, facing defeat at Philippi, both committed suicide. The situation then degenerated into a rivalry between the armies of Mark Antony and Octavius, with Octavius emerging victorious. It had been 13 years since Julius Caesar's death. Octavius, also called Caesar Augustus, had become the first emperor of the Roman Empire.

The defeated Mark Antony went home to Cleopatra, whom he had married in 37 B.C. Together, they committed suicide. Cleopatra had arranged for her son, now 16, to escape, but Octavius had him murdered. Lepidus, the third member of the triumvirate, had been ineffectual and unimportant. He retired to the priesthood, where he apparently spent most of his time drinking.

### *Activity #2: Thinking About the Facts: Does History Really Repeat Itself?*
Students have probably heard the phrase, "History repeats itself." Have them look over their fact sheets and see if they can draw any parallels between Roman political figures and events and those of today. To get them started thinking, ask:

1. Do you think Caesar was a "ladies' man"? Can you think of any powerful figures in today's world who have this reputation?
2. How was the set-up of the original government of the republic similar to ours?
3. Voters in the Roman popular assemblies were influenced to vote a certain way by those who were powerful. Does this ever happen in our country?
4. Caesar, Pompey, and Octavius were all military heroes who rose to power after winning wars. Think back through American history. How many similar instances can you name? (List on the board.)

Name_____                                    *Julius Caesar*
                                                                 Prereading Activity #1

# Fact Sheet: The Roman Republic

The Roman Republic gained supremacy in _____. The two chief magistrates in Roman government were called _____. The Romans who had most of the power were the _____, but the _____ could also hold office. As the republic of Rome defeated all of the countries surrounding it, the generals and Senators shared the _____ and became more and more wealthy. Other sources of their wealth were the _____ paid by the defeated countries and the _____ offered to them by people who wanted them to grant them favors or vote a certain way. Even the members of the _____ _____ accepted money for votes. Many _____ _____ sold their land to the wealthy and moved to the city of _____, where they ran out of money and joined the ranks of the unemployed. The first triumvirate was formed by _____, _____, and _____ in _____ B.C. Then _____ died, and civil war broke out. _____ defeated _____ in _____ B.C. In 44 B.C., he was assassinated by _____, _____, and other members of a conspiracy whose members felt he was too powerful. After the murder of _____, a second triumvirate was formed. It included _____, _____, and _____. Its members vowed to _____.

**The background information can be given to students as a lecture. Be sure to advise them that questions about Shakespeare will appear on the final exam.**

# William Shakespeare

One of the great mysteries of English drama is that so little is known for sure about one of its most famous playwrights. Fact became mingled with legend in the 100 years after Shakespeare's death, and it was not until then that any biographical information was recorded.

Shakespeare's exact birthdate is unknown, but he was baptized on April 26, 1564, in Stratford-on-Avon, England. His father, John, was a prosperous wool, leather, and grain merchant as well as a town official. His mother, Mary, was the daughter of a gentleman farmer. It is known that young William attended school and studied Latin and literature. In 1582, he married Anne Hathaway, a woman eight years his senior. They had three children: a daughter, Susanna, and twins Hamnet and Judeth.

In 1586, Shakespeare left Stratford to become the stage manager of The Theatre in London, so named because it was the only theatre in town. He soon joined the acting company of The Theatre, and with Richard Burbage and William Kemp he performed at court in many plays.

Shakespeare's earliest works were produced in 1591-1592, including several of the histories and *Love's Labour's Lost, Two Gentlemen of Verona*, and *Comedy of Errors*. In 1592, he wrote *Romeo and Juliet*. It was followed in quick succession by *The Merchant of Venice, A Midsummer Night's Dream, All's Well That Ends Well, The Taming of the Shrew*, and *The Merry Wives of Windsor*.

Shakespeare made an important business move in 1599 when he joined Richard Burbage and several other actors and built the Globe Theatre. He was a shareholder in the Globe and a part-owner of a company of actors called Lord Chamberlain's Company, later known as The King's Men.

Many of Shakespeare's plays were produced at the Globe, where he had both financial security and a first-rate acting company to produce his plays. This was his greatest writing period. In 1599-1600 he wrote *Much Ado About Nothing, As You Like It*, and *Twelfth Night*. Between 1600 and 1611, he wrote the tragedies for which he is so well remembered: *Julius Caesar, Hamlet, Othello, Macbeth, King Lear*, and *Antony and Cleopatra*, among others. During this time he also wrote 154 sonnets which were published in 1609. Late in 1608 or 1609, Shakespeare and his partners purchased the Blackfriars Theatre to use as a winter location for play production.

In 1611, at the height of his fame and popularity, Shakespeare moved back to Stratford. His son died at this time. He sold out his interests in London, although he did continue to write and travel to the city until his death in 1616.

# The Globe Theatre

Obtain a picture of the Globe Theatre to show your class, or obtain an educational kit and build a small model so students can see the various areas of the theatre as they are discussed in class.

## Physical Aspects

The Globe had three levels open to the sky and set on a large platform. The stage jutted out into the audience on three sides. The building itself was octagon-shaped (eight sides). A cross-section of the London population attended. For one cent, a theatre-goer could stand or sit on the ground and would be referred to as a "groundling." Two cents would buy a seat in the galleries and elsewhere. The noblemen paid nothing, and were seated in the lord's rooms near the stage. Plays were always performed during the day, as there were no lights. A flag was flown on top of the theatre on days when a play would be given.

## Setting/Staging

The plays performed at the Globe Theatre had little or no interruption. There were no curtains to signal the end of an act, although there was a tiring house, a room where actors could change costumes or stay out of view when they were not on stage. The settings were given through action and dialogue. The actors' soliloquies made the audience feel particularly involved, as the actors seemed to be talking directly to the audience. Actors' entrances and exits were seen openly by the audience through two doors on either side of the stage.

## The Actors

Senior actors got the major parts in plays. They were experienced and often held shares in the theatre company. Hired men, who were paid weekly and held no shares, held backstage jobs and played minor parts in the plays. Boy actors played the roles of women and children.

---

**Review questions for students to answer from notes**

1. What are Shakespeare's birthplace and year of birth?
2. In what ways did Shakespeare participate in drama?
3. With what type of plays is Shakespeare credited?
4. During what Age did Shakespeare live?
5. What theatre in London did Shakespeare help organize?
6. What classes of people came to see the plays?
7. Were there any elaborate settings in Shakespeare's theatre?
8. Who played the parts of women and children?
9. When and where did Shakespeare die?

Name_____  *Julius Caesar*
Prereading Activity #3

# Drama Terms

1. act
2. comedy
3. dialogue
4. tragedy
5. melodrama
6. protagonist
7. antagonist
8. theme
9. climax
10. plot
11. stage left
12. stage right
13. rising action
14. falling action
15. exposition
16. crisis

Name_____

*Julius Caesar*
Drama Terms Quiz

**Matching:** Place the correct letter next to each description.

_____ 1. The central unifying idea of a play which underlies plot, action, and dialogue.

_____ 2. The introductory section of a play in which characters, time, place, and situation are presented.

_____ 3. The high point in the action of the play.

_____ 4. Term used to refer to the left of the stage from the actor's point of view.

_____ 5. The series of events following the highest dramatic point.

_____ 6. A play designed to arouse immediate and intense emotion by means of exaggeration and fast-moving action.

_____ 7. The hero or leading character with whom the audience sympathizes. The "good guy."

_____ 8. The main story of the play; the series of situations and incidents through which the characters move, thereby telling a story.

_____ 9. Conversation between at least two characters.

_____ 10. Character who opposes or conflicts with another. The "bad guy."

A. act
B. comedy
C. dialogue
D. tragedy
E. melodrama
F. protagonist
G. antagonist
H. theme
I. climax
J. plot
K. rising action
L. falling action
M. stage right
N. exposition
O. stage left
P. crisis

Name_____

*Julius Caesar*
Study Questions

Write a brief answer to each study question as you read the play at home or in class. When you study for the final exam, use the questions for review.

**Introduction**
1. What event in Caesar's career immediately preceded the play's action?
2. Give the date of the assassination of Caesar.

**ACT I**
*Scene i*
1. What is a tribune?
2. Why do Flavius and Marullus want the commoners to disperse? Why do they remove the garlands from Caesar's statue?

*Scene ii*
1. Why does Caesar tell Calpurnia to stand close to the racers so Antony can touch her?
2. How does Cassius feel about Caesar? What does he want Brutus to do?
3. How does Caesar feel about Cassius?
4. Why does the crowd cheer during this scene?
5. What physical disabilities does Caesar have?
6. What does Cassius conclude about Brutus?

*Scene iii*
1. When does this scene take place?
2. What strange omens are seen?
3. What is learned about the conspiracy against Caesar in this scene?

**ACT II**
*Scene i*
1. What is the meaning of Brutus' speech, lines 10-34?
2. Why is no oath sworn by the conspirators?
3. Why is Cicero left out of the conspiracy?
4. Why does Brutus not want Antony killed?
5. How does Decius plan to persuade Caesar to go to the Capitol?
6. How does Portia show Brutus she can be trusted? Will he tell her his secrets?

*Scene ii*
1. What omens frighten Calpurnia?
2. Is she successful in persuading Caesar not to go to the Senate?
3. Why does he change his mind?

*Scene iii*
1. What is Artemidorus planning to do?

Name_____

*Julius Caesar*
Study Questions—page 2

*Scene iv*
1. What are Portia's feelings in this scene?

## ACT III
*Scene i*
1. What two warnings does Caesar ignore?
2. What was the specific task each of the following had to perform in order to execute the slaying?
    a. Metellus Cimber
    b. Casca
    c. Trebonius
3. How does Metellus Cimber get Caesar's attention?
4. What do we learn about Caesar's character from his reply to Metellus Cimber?
5. What is significant about Caesar's famous line, "Et tu Brute?" immediately before he dies?
6. What happens immediately after Caesar is killed?
7. Is Antony honest when he speaks to the conspirators? How do you know?
8. Who is coming to Rome? What advice does Antony give?

*Scene ii*
1. Does Brutus appeal to the emotions or the reasoning powers of the crowd?
2. What reason does Brutus give for the murder of Caesar?
3. What word does Antony emphasize in his speech? Why?
4. How does Antony use "reverse psychology" in talking to the crowd?
5. Describe the crowd's reaction after both speeches. What does this tell you about the crowd in general?
6. How does Antony entice the crowd to listen to him?

*Scene iii*
1. What is the purpose of this scene?

## ACT IV
*Scene i*
1. What three men make up the new triumvirate?
2. What are they doing as the scene opens?
3. What opinion does Antony have of Lepidus?

*Scene ii*
1. Where does this scene take place?
2. What feelings exist between Brutus and Cassius?

*Scene iii*
1. What are the reasons behind the quarrel between Brutus and Cassius?
2. How does the quarrel end?

Name_____

*Julius Caesar*
Study Questions—page 3

3. What has happened to Portia?
4. Why does Cassius want to be on the defensive and wait to be attacked where they are camped?
5. What is Brutus' reason for wanting to take the offensive and march to Philippi?
6. Which strategy is decided upon? Why?
7. Why does Brutus have Varro and Claudius sleep in his tent?
8. What premonition does Brutus have of his death?
9. What "visitor" does Brutus have in the night? What warning does he receive?

**ACT V**
*Scene i*
1. Where does the action in this scene occur? How is this important to the play?
2. What lines imply that there will be results by the end of the day?
3. What are Cassius' thoughts of the future?
4. What does Brutus imply he will do if he sees that he is losing?

*Scene ii*
1. What prompted Brutus to send Messala with a message to the troops?

*Scene iii*
1. What does Pindarus report to Cassius?
2. How does Cassius die?
3. Who had actually surrounded Titinius?
4. What is the meaning of Brutus' lines, "O Julius Caesar, Thou art mighty yet!"

*Scene iv*
1. What action in the scene shows you that Brutus' men respect and protect him?

*Scene v*
1. How does the action in this scene add to the idea shown in scene iv?
2. Of what glory does Brutus speak in line 36?
3. Explain the meaning of Brutus' final speech, lines 50-51.
4. Explain Antony's final speech, lines 68-75.
5. What is the mood of the final scene?

Name_____

*Julius Caesar*
Vocabulary List

Look up the following words in your book's glossary, the text footnotes, or the dictionary. Choose the meaning that best fits the context of the play, and write it next to the word on a separate sheet of paper. The numbers next to the words are the lines where you will find them in the play.

## ACT I

*Scene i*

knave 15
concave 48
plague 55

*Scene ii*

hinder 30
countenance 38
cogitations 50
lamented 55
chafing 101
doublet 261

*Scene iii*

saucy 12
portentous 31
construe 34

## ACT II

*Scene i*

adder 14
base (adj.) 26
redress 57
visage 81
affability 82
interpose 98
sufferance 115
lottery 119
harlot 287
exploit 317

*Scene ii*

valiant 33
augurers 38
entrails 39
lusty 78
amiss 83

*Scene iv*

ere 5
comment 43

## ACT III

*Scene i*

puissant 33
couchings 36
repealing 51
enfranchisement 57
Olympus 74
credit 191
conceit 192
corse 199
Havoc 273

*Scene ii*

lovers 13
extenuated 40
coffers 91
meet (adj.) 151
vesture 198

## ACT IV

*Scene i*

provender 30
corporal 33
covert 46

*Scene ii*

mettle 24
jades 26

*Scene iii*

vaunting 52
rived 83
insupportable 150
taper 163

## ACT V

*Scene iii*

disconsolate 55
misconstrue 84

Name_____

*Julius Caesar*
Vocabulary Quiz 1
Act I

**Fill in the blanks with the appropriate vocabulary word from Act I.**

| | | | |
|---|---|---|---|
| plague | cogitations | doublet | construe |
| knave | concave | hinder | lamented |
| portentous | countenance | | |

1. "Have you not made an universal shout,/ That Tiber trembled underneath her banks/ To hear the replication of your sounds/ Made in her _____ shores?"

2. "If I have veiled my look,/ I turn the trouble of my _____/ Merely upon myself."

3. "And it is very much _____, Brutus,/ That you have no such mirrors as will turn/ Your hidden worthiness into your eye,/ That you might see your shadow."

4. "For I believe they are _____ things Unto the climate that they point upon."

5. "Marry, before he fell down, when he perceived the common herd was glad he refused the crown, he plucked me ope his _____ and offered them his throat to cut."

6. "Then, Brutus, I have much mistook your passion,/ By means whereof this breast of mine hath buried/ Thoughts of great value, worthy _____."

7. "Pray to the gods to intermit the _____ That needs must light on this ingratitude."

8. "Let me not _____, Cassius, your desires;/ I'll leave you."

9. "Indeed it is a strange-disposed time: But men may _____ things after their fashion."

Name_____

*Julius Caesar*
Vocabulary Quiz 2
Acts II and III

**Fill in the blanks with the appropriate vocabulary word from Acts II and III.**

affability  vesture  redress  sufferance
puissant  harlot  coffers  adder
couchings  enfranchisement

1. "If the _____ will follow, thou receivest
   Thy full petition at the hand of Brutus!"

2. "… If it be no more, Portia is Brutus' _____, not his wife."

3. "…If not the face of men,/
   The _____ of our souls, the time's abuse—/
   If these be motives weak, break off betimes,/ And every man hence to his idle bed."

4. "How might that change his nature, there's the question./ It is the bright day that brings forth the _____, And that craves wary walking."

5. "…Seek none, Conspiracy—
   / Hide it in smiles and _____."

6. "Most high, most mighty, and most _____ Caesar,/
   Metellus Cimber throws before thy seat/ An humble heart."

7. "As low as to thy foot doth Cassius fall
   To beg _____ for Publius Cimber."

8. "He hath brought many captives home to Rome,/
   Whose ransoms did the general _____ fill."

9. "Kind souls, what weep you when you but behold/
   Our Caesar's _____ wounded?"

Name_____

*Julius Caesar*
Vocabulary Quiz 3
Acts IV and V

**Fill in the blanks with the appropriate vocabulary word from Acts IV and V.**

misconstrued   vaunting   rived   provender
covert   mettle   corporal   taper
disconsolate   insupportable

1. "So is my horse, Octavius, and for that I do appoint him store of
   _____."

2. "And let us presently go sit in council
   How _____ matters may be best disclosed,
   And open perils surest answered."

3. "But hollow men, like horses hot at hand,
   Make gallant show and promise of their _____;"

4. "You say you are a better soldier: Let it appear so; Make your
   _____ true, And it shall please me well."

5. "All _____, with Pindarus his bondman on this hill."

6. "Did I not meet thy friends, and did not they
   Put on my brows this wreath of victory,
   And bid me give it thee? Didst thou not hear their shouts?
   Alas, thou hast _____ everything!"

7. "I did not. He was but a fool
   That brought my answer back.
   Brutus hath _____ my heart."

Name_____

Julius Caesar
Act I Quiz

**Short Answer.**

1. Who warned Caesar concerning the ides of March?

2. Give two examples of omens of chaos at the beginning of scene three.

3. What is the "…enterprise/ Of honorable dangerous consequence" to which Cassius refers?

4. What was the Roman belief concerning a barren woman and the Lupercalia holiday?

**Matching:** Write the letter of the character's name next to the correct description.

____ 5. originator of the conspiracy

____ 6. Caesar's wife

____ 7. a wise old senator

____ 8. a tribune who berates the commoners

____ 9. recently defeated by Caesar

____ 10. a man the conspiracy hopes will join them

| | |
|---|---|
| a. | Cicero |
| b. | Casca |
| c. | Flavius |
| d. | Calpurnia |
| e. | Cassius |
| f. | Pompey |
| g. | Brutus |

**Quotes.** Identify the speaker and listener.

11. "Into what dangers would you lead me, ———,/ That you would have me seek into myself/ For that which is not in me?"

_____ to _____

12. "Yond Cassius has a lean and hungry look; He thinks too much; such men are dangerous."

_____ to _____

Name_____

*Julius Caesar*
Act II Quiz

**Short Answer.**

1. What did Lucius bring to Brutus?

2. Brutus' soliloquy in his orchard is about what?

3. What things cause Calpurnia to urge Caesar not to leave the house?

4. Whom does Cassius want to kill in addition to Caesar?

**Identify each character.**

5. Brutus' servant _____

6. convinces Caesar to go to the Capitol _____

7. advises conspiracy not to include Cicero _____

8. tells Brutus he should reveal his secrets to her _____

9. writes a warning letter to Caesar _____

10. Name at least four of the conspirators: _____, _____, _____, _____.

**Explain in your own words what each quote means. Identify the speaker.**

11. "Cowards die many times before their deaths;
    The valiant never taste of death but once."

    Speaker:

    Meaning:

12. "It is the bright day that brings forth the adder,/ And that craves wary walking."

    Speaker:

    Meaning:

Name_____                              *Julius Caesar*
                                                          Act III Quiz

**Short Answer.**

1. What did Trebonius do to assist in Caesar's murder?

2. Who was the first to stab Caesar? The last?

3. What does Antony's soliloquy over Caesar's body tell us about his loyalties?

| A. Mark Antony | C. Metellus | E. Cinna | G. Brutus |
| B. the crowd   | D. Casca    | F. Caesar |          |

**Next to each quote, write the letter of the character who said it.**

_____ 4. "Et tu, Brute?"
_____ 5. "Why, he that cuts off twenty years of life
          Cuts off so many years of fearing death."
_____ 6. "To you our swords have leaden points, Mark Antony…"
_____ 7. "Woe to the hand that shed this costly blood!"
_____ 8. "Not that I loved Caesar less, but that I loved Rome more."
_____ 9. "'Tis good you know not that you are his heirs;
          For if you should, O, what would come of it?"
_____ 10. "Peace, ho! Hear Antony, most noble Antony!"
_____ 11. "I am _____ the poet! I am _____ the poet!"
_____ 12. "Is there no voice more worthy than my own,
          To sound more sweetly in great Caesar's ear
          For the repealing of my banished brother?"

**Essay.** Choose either Brutus' or Antony's funeral oration for Caesar, and summarize what was said and how the crowd reacted.

Name_____

*Julius Caesar*
Act IV Quiz

**Short Answer.**

1. Who are the members of the new triumvirate?

2. In the conversation between them, of what does Brutus accuse Cassius?

3. What disturbing visitor visits Brutus, and what warning does he give?

4. In addition to anger, Brutus is also feeling grief. Why?

**For each quote, explain the circumstances or reason for the character's lines, identify the speaker, and paraphrase the meaning.**

5. "A friend should bear his friend's infirmities,
   But _____ makes mine greater than they are."
   Speaker:
   Circumstances:
   Meaning:

6. "This is a slight unmeritable man,
   Meet to be sent on errands…"
   Speaker:
   Circumstances:
   Meaning:

7. "…Ha! Who comes here?
   I think it is the weakness of mine eyes
   That shapes this monstrous apparition."
   Speaker:
   Circumstances:
   Meaning:

Name_____

*Julius Caesar*
Act V Quiz

**Short Answer.**

1. What crucial mistake did Pindarus make in this act?

2. What omens caused Cassius to be doubtful of victory?

3. How did Cassius die?

4. How did Brutus die?

**Match the letter next to each character with his action or description.**

_____ 5. died on his birthday

_____ 6. called Brutus "the noblest Roman of them all"

_____ 7. rode down to see if soldiers were friends or foes

_____ 8. held Brutus' sword for him

_____ 9. tried to impersonate Brutus

_____ 10. urged Brutus to escape immediately

_____ 11. proclaimed that Brutus would have a proper burial

a. Lucilius
b. Cassius
c. Clitus
d. Octavius
e. Mark Antony
f. Strato
g. Titinius
h. Caesar
i. Pindarus

**Identify the speaker.**

12. "Caesar, now be still;/ I killed not thee with half so good a will."

    _____

13. "…Caesar, thou art revenged,/ Even with the sword that killed thee."

    _____

14. "All the conspirators save only he/ Did that they did in envy of great Caesar."

    _____

Name_____

Julius Caesar
Act I Activity

Much of *Julius Caesar* was written in blank verse in *iambic pentameter*. Blank verse does not rhyme, but each line has the same number of stressed and unstressed syllables. When the lines are written in iambic pentameter, it means there are five sets (called <u>feet</u>) of two syllables each, with the accent on the second syllable.

Here is an example of rhymed iambic pentameter from Shakespeare's *Sonnet 14*.

*To <u>me</u>,/ fair <u>Friend</u>, / you <u>ne</u>/ ver <u>can</u> / be <u>old</u>,*

*For as you were when first your eye I eyed*

*Such seems your beauty still. Three winters cold*

*Have from the forests shook three summers' pride;*

The first line is divided into iambic feet by the / marks, and the stressed syllables are underlined.

- **Mark the rest of the poem the same way.**
- **Show the rhyme scheme by writing "A" or "B" at the ends of lines.**

Below are some lines from *Julius Caesar*.

*I would not, Cassius, yet I love him well.*
*But wherefore do you hold me here so long?*
*What is it that you would impart to me?*
*If it be aught toward the general good,...*

- **Mark these lines as you did the ones above.**

- **What do these lines have in common with the lines from the sonnet?**

- **How are these lines different from the lines from the sonnet?**

© Novel Units, Inc.                                                                                       All rights reserved

Name_____

*Julius Caesar*
Act II Activity

## Picturing Portia, Cutting Out Calpurnia…

For this assignment, you'll need some old magazines or newspapers and your copy of *Julius Caesar*.

The characters in the play are not actually described in words, as they would be in a novel or short story. Your own imagination must supply descriptions, so your friend's Caesar and Brutus and Cassius may not look anything like yours.

1. Look through your magazines and/or newspapers and locate pictures of people you feel look something like your imagination's pictures of Caesar, Brutus, Cassius, Portia, and Calpurnia.

2. Cut out the five pictures you like the best. Glue or tape them to separate pieces of plain white paper or construction paper.

3. Choose a line or a few lines from the play for each character, and write them under their corresponding pictures.

© Novel Units, Inc.    All rights reserved

*Julius Caesar*
Act III Activities

**Choose one of the following activities.**

1. Shakespeare didn't write a scene depicting how Calpurnia reacted to the news of her husband's death. Imagine that she and a good friend are chatting in the garden when a servant brings the bad news. Work with two other students to write and present the scene.

2. Work with a group to present the first scene of **Act III through line 77** (Caesar's death). One person can read the lines of Artemidorus, the Soothsayer, Publius, Popilius, and Casca. You will need one student each to play Caesar, Cassius, Brutus, Decius, Cinna, and Metellus.

3. Memorize one of the following speeches and present it to the class:

   **Act III, scene i:**

   lines 148-163 - Antony's speech to the conspirators

   lines 164-176 - Brutus' reply to Antony

   lines 254-275 - Antony's soliloquy over Caesar's body

   **Act III, scene ii:**

   lines 12-35 - Brutus' speech to the citizens

   lines 74-108 - Antony's speech to the citizens

   lines 120-139 - Antony's speech to the citizens

   lines 171-199 - Antony's speech to the citizens

   lines 212-232 - Antony's speech to the citizens

© Novel Units, Inc.                          All rights reserved

Name_____

*Julius Caesar*
Act IV Activity

**Cassius told Brutus, "A friend should bear his friend's infirmities."**

Make a list below of your "infirmities"— the little things about yourself that your family and friends might find irritating at times. Then make a list of <u>their</u> infirmities. How well do you bear them?

**My Infirmities**




**Infirmities of Family and Friends
Which I'm Trying to Overlook or Understand**
(Do not include names.)

Name_____

*Julius Caesar*
Act V Activity

## What if ...

In drama, as in other written works, events are caused by certain actions or other events. The cause leads to an effect, which then becomes a cause of another effect, and so on. Since *Julius Caesar* is based on historical fact, Shakespeare had most of his plot when he began writing. If the play had been entirely made up of fictitious events, however, the outcome could have changed at many points. Consider each of the following changes in plot, and briefly describe how each might affect the other events and outcome of the play.

1. Instead of ignoring the soothsayer, Caesar has a long talk with him about why he should beware the ides of March.

2. Brutus tells Portia all about his secret plans as soon as she asks.

3. Caesar is too frightened by Calpurnia's dream to leave the house.

4. Brutus refuses to go along with the conspiracy, and tells Caesar about it.

5. The citizens don't bother to listen to Antony's speech.

6. Pindarus brings back the message that the men surrounding Titinius are Brutus' victorious soldiers.

Name_____

*Julius Caesar*
Review Activity #1

**Match the Shakespearean language on the left with the modern language on the right.**

_____ 1. "Nor construe any further my neglect
Than that poor Brutus, with himself at war,
Forgets the shows of love to other men."

_____ 2. "The angry spot doth glow on Caesar's brow."

_____ 3. "Oh he sits high in all the people's hearts,
And that which would appear offense in us,
His countenance, like richest alchemy,
Will change to virtue and to worthiness."

_____ 4. "Shall I entreat a word?"

_____ 5. "I cannot tell what you and other men
Think of this life, but for my single self
I had as lief not be as live to be
In awe of such a thing as I myself."

_____ 6. "Run to the Capitol, and nothing else?
And so return to you, nothing else?"

_____ 7. "Most mighty Caesar, let me know some cause, Lest I be laughed at when I tell them so."

_____ 8. "Caesar doth bear me hard, but he loves Brutus."

_____ 9. "The secrets of my heart,
All my engagements I will construe to thee,
All the charactery of my sad brows."

_____ 10. "...for his silver hairs
Will purchase us a good opinion,
And buy men's voices to commend our deeds."

A. I don't know about you, but I would rather die than have to be a servant to another man as good as I.

B. Wow, Caesar is really mad.

C. I know Caesar doesn't like me, but he does like Brutus.

D. You may have misinterpreted.

E. Without Brutus, we will look like villains; with him, patriots.

F. He is old and wise, and by placing him on our side, we will gain the support of the people.

G. I'll tell you my troubles in a moment.

H. Don't be upset! I just have so much on my mind that I'm not paying attention to anyone.

I. Let me know why, so the others don't think I'm lying or joking.

J. You just want me to go back and forth for *no* reason?

Name_____

*Julius Caesar*
Review Activity #2

**Put the events below in chronological sequence by numbering them 1-16.**

_____   The conspirators kill Caesar.

_____   Brutus joins the conspiracy.

_____   Calpurnia tells Caesar about her frightening dream.

_____   Tribunes berate citizens for cheering Caesar.

_____   Antony talks with the conspirators.

_____   Portia begs Brutus to tell her what he's up to.

_____   Cassius receives false information, and asks Pindarus to kill him.

_____   Antony speaks to the citizens.

_____   A soothsayer tells Caesar to beware the ides of March.

_____   Caesar's ghost appears to Brutus.

_____   Antony reveals his true feelings over Caesar's body.

_____   Brutus kills himself.

_____   Brutus speaks to the citizens.

_____   Brutus and Cassius leave Rome as Octavius arrives.

_____   The conspirators plan a way to get Brutus to join them.

_____   Antony calls Brutus "the noblest Roman of them all."

# Essay Topic Suggestions

1. In what way does the crowd function as a character in Julius Caesar?
2. One thing Caesar and Brutus have in common is their divided selves. Compare the two characters with special reference to their public and private selves.
3. Shakespeare often used imagery to create "mental pictures" in the mind's eyes of his audience. Give examples of this imagery.
4. Compare and contrast the scene between Portia and Brutus with the scenes between Caesar and Calpurnia.
5. Compare and contrast either of the following: Antony and Brutus; Cassius and Brutus.
6. Flattery is a tool used a number of times by characters in Julius Caesar. Give examples.
7. Compare and contrast the funeral orations for Caesar given by Brutus and Antony.
8. Define dramatic irony and give examples from the play.
9. Did Shakespeare provide credible motivation for the important steps taken by each of his major characters? Support your answer with details and examples.
10. What is the dominant theme of Julius Caesar? Support your opinion with details and examples.
11. What are the major events leading to Brutus' downfall?
12. Discuss Brutus as a naïve idealist.
13. Discuss Cassius as a brilliant strategist.

# Ideas for Projects

1. As a research project, have students find out more about Julius Caesar and what actually happened during and shortly after his lifetime. They might then compare historical fact with Shakespeare's representation.
2. As an art/geography project, have a student draw a poster-size map of the Roman Empire in 44 B.C. This project can be assigned at the beginning of the unit so the map can be used as a visual aid.
3. As a drama project, have groups of students enact and videotape a soliloquy or a particular scene. This should be done as an outside project, but the finished video can be shown to the class.
4. Many famous sayings come from Shakespeare's plays. Have a student research these and write them on 6" wide strips of poster board that can then be placed around the room.
5. As an art/literature project, have a student draw a cartoon strip depicting an important scene from the play.

Name_____

*Julius Caesar*
Final Exam
Advanced Level

## Essay Questions for Examination

1. The influence of Julius Caesar on other principal characters is a major force in Shakespeare's play. Antony worships him as a man and as a power. Brutus admires him as a man but fears him as a power. Cassius despises him as a man and therefore as a power. Select ONE of these three characters, and write an essay clearly showing the character's attitude toward Caesar by using examples and details as evidence.

2. Brutus makes several errors in judgment. List three and explain why they are errors.

3. Brutus is the main character of the play. It is his personal tragedy that is lived out during the play. Keeping this in mind, justify the title of the play.

4. What purpose is served by letting Octavius make the final speech of the play?

5. What is the reason for the introduction of Caesar's ghost into the play?

6. Can Cassius also be seen as a tragic figure? Support your opinion.

Name_____

*Julius Caesar*
Final Exam
Objective Questions

## Background Information

1. If you ever visited England, you'd probably want to visit the town of Shakespeare's birth and death, which is
   - a. London
   - b. Warwick-on-the-Lake
   - c. Birmingham-on-Thames
   - d. Stratford-on-Avon

2. Shakespeare participated in drama by
   - a. writing plays
   - b. acting
   - c. partially financing his plays
   - d. all of these

3. With what type of play(s) is Shakespeare credited?
   - a. tragedies
   - b. comedies
   - c. histories
   - d. mysteries
   - e. a, b, and c

4. Shakespeare lived during the _____ Age.
   - a. Victorian
   - b. Medieval
   - c. Elizabethan
   - d. Romantic

5. William Shakespeare's life spans the following dates:
   - a. 44 A.D.-100
   - b. 1803-1868
   - c. 1564-1616
   - d. 1720-1776

6. The theatre in which most of Shakespeare's plays were acted was
   - a. Blackstone
   - b. Universal
   - c. Arie Crown
   - d. Globe

7. Most play audiences consisted of
   - a. only upper class people
   - b. only poor people
   - c. only men and boys
   - d. rich and poor alike

8. Women's parts were portrayed by
   - a. women of the upper class only
   - b. young boys
   - c. slaves
   - d. girls who auditioned for the parts

9. Most historians believe that the stage of the theatre used by Shakespeare
   - a. projected out into the audience
   - b. had curtains all around it
   - c. was quite far removed from the audience
   - d. contained a large amount of scenery

© Novel Units, Inc.  All rights reserved

Name_____

Julius Caesar
Final Exam—Objective Questions
page 2

10. One limitation of a playwright in Shakespeare's time was
    a. the audiences were too small to support a writer
    b. only men of the upper class could write plays
    c. almost the entire setting had to be related through the dialogue of the characters
    d. only writers approved by the church could have plays performed

11. Other than being a famous political figure, the real-life Julius Caesar is also known for his conquest of
    a. Gaul         b. Syria
    c. Egypt        d. Greece

12. Caesar became the most important man in Rome only after
    a. he won Syria for the glory of Rome
    b. a bloody civil war against Pompey
    c. he arose as a ghost
    d. Cicero convinced the Senate Caesar was a good leader

13. In 45 B.C., the real Julius Caesar appointed himself
    a. the top man in the triumvirate    b. Consul for a year
    c. a Senator                          d. dictator for life

14. The action of the play begins in the year
    a. 44 B.C.      b. 44 A.D.
    c. 1564 A.D.    d. 1599 A.D.

**Matching**

Match the character with his/her appropriate description. No letter is used twice, but there are some letters which are not used.

    a. Artemidorus      ab. Calpurnia      bd. Ligarius
    b. Octavius         ac. Pindarus       be. Cassius
    c. Lepidus          ad. Caesar         cd. Decius
    d. Mark Antony      ae. Titinius       ce. Casca
    e. Portia           bc. Brutus

_____ 15. has a dream about a statue

_____ 16. tries to give Caesar a note about conspiracy

_____ 17. has Rome's honor and future in mind <u>always</u>

Name_____

Julius Caesar
Final Exam—Objective Questions
page 3

_____ 18. one who gives tribute to Brutus over his body

_____ 19. joins the conspiracy without knowing what it is

_____ 20. one who bears the scar of a self-inflicted wound

_____ 21. is a gossip, and tells of Caesar's refusal of the crown

_____ 22. the new triumvirate member Antony hopes to get rid of

_____ 23. dies on birthday

_____ 24. kills himself/herself because Cassius is dead

## Julius Caesar

25. Caesar's two physical defects were
   a. crippled left leg, deafness
   b. deafness, falling sickness
   c. falling sickness, nausea
   d. weak eyesight, obesity

26. When Brutus says, "Set honor in one eye and death in the other and I will look on both indifferently," he means
   a. his eyes are giving him trouble
   b. if an act is honorable and for the public benefit, Brutus will do it in spite of personal consequences
   c. if a plan will benefit Brutus, he will consider it
   d. he doesn't care much what they do

27. Brutus goes through extreme mental torment or inner conflict trying to decide whether or not he should kill Caesar. Why is this?
   a. Brutus fears he will not have the courage to stab Caesar.
   b. Brutus is torn between his ideals and his personal liking for Caesar.
   c. Brutus fears someone will reveal the plot to Caesar.
   d. Brutus thinks that Cassius might gain power for himself.

28. Which of the following is Brutus' reason for killing Caesar?
   a. Brutus is jealous of Caesar's power.
   b. Caesar has rebuked him, and Brutus wants revenge.
   c. Brutus is afraid of the type of ruler Caesar will become.
   d. Brutus does not like the type of ruler Caesar has been.

29. Why does Brutus not insist on an oath between the conspirators?
   a. He prefers a written contract.
   b. He believes their motives are sufficient and that they are all honorable.
   c. Cassius does not think an oath is necessary.
   d. Brutus fears if they make an oath, Caesar will hear of it.

Name_____

*Julius Caesar*
Final Exam—Objective Questions
page 4

30. Which of the lines below states the reason why some of the conspirators think Cicero should be included in the plottings?
    a. "Such men as he be never at heart's ease."
    b. "His silver hairs will purchase us a good opinion."
    c. "We shall find him a shrewd contriver."
    d. "Caesar doth bear him hard for speaking ill of Pompey."

31. Which character does Brutus think is weak and powerless, but who proves to be the opposite?
    a. Julius Caesar
    b. Antony
    c. Calpurnia
    d. Cinna the Poet

32. How does Decius say he will get Caesar to the Capitol?
    a. through bribery
    b. through physical force
    c. through reasoning
    d. through flattery

33. After the assassination plot has begun, who eventually takes over the leadership of the conspiracy?
    a. Antony
    b. Brutus
    c. Cassius
    d. Cicero

34. All of the following are examples of warnings based on superstitious belief **except**
    a. the soothsayer's warning
    b. Calpurnia's dream
    c. the "beast without a heart"
    d. Artemidorus' petition

35. In Calpurnia's interpretation of her dream, the bleeding Caesar symbolizes
    a. a dead Caesar
    b. a Caesar giving Rome reviving blood
    c. Caesar having an epileptic fit
    d. Caesar leading his army to Philippi

36. What pretense do the conspirators use to get near Caesar to stab him?
    a. a shout that scatters the Senators
    b. a petition by Metellus Cimber about his exiled brother
    c. flattery to which Caesar has always been susceptible

37. What conspirator gives Caesar the "unkindest cut of all"?
    a. Cassius
    b. Brutus
    c. Casca
    d. Metellus Cimber

38. Why does Caesar stop struggling against the conspirators?
    a. He is too weak.
    b. He sees how many there are.
    c. He sees Brutus among them.
    d. He realizes his own errors.

Name_____

*Julius Caesar*
Final Exam—Objective Questions
page 5

39. When does Antony reveal his true feelings after Caesar's death?
    a. when he shakes hands with the conspirators
    b. when he sends his servant to talk to Brutus
    c. when he is left alone with Caesar's body
    d. when he agrees to follow the wishes of the conspirators

40. When Antony asked to deliver a funeral oration, who was suspicious?
    a. Casca
    b. Brutus
    c. Cassius
    d. Lepidus

41. Shakespeare used prose rather than poetry for the crowd's speeches because
    a. the crowd is emotional
    b. the crowd is rational
    c. the crowd is base
    d. prose is easier to read than poetry
    e. all of the above

42. What word in Antony's funeral oration is ironically used over and over?
    a. Brutus
    b. worthy
    c. honorable
    d. Caesar

43. When the new triumvirate is formed, Antony shows his ruthlessness and ambition by
    a. plotting to kill the other triumvirs
    b. denouncing Brutus once again to the crowd
    c. condemning to death all who oppose the new triumvirate
    d. proclaiming himself Emperor of Rome

44. "This is a slight, unmeritable man, Meet to be sent on errands;" shows that the relationship between Antony and his partners is one of
    a. distrust and lack of respect
    b. unanimous agreement
    c. humorous give and take
    d. cordiality

45. One apparent reason for Brutus' and Cassius' quarrel is that
    a. Brutus wanted to free all the slaves, while Cassius wanted to keep Messala
    b. Brutus accuses Cassius of being greedy and money-hungry
    c. Brutus is naturally quarrelsome
    d. Caesar's ghost has been keeping Brutus awake nights

46. In the quarrel scene between Cassius and Brutus and in their death scenes, we find that a continuing influence on both is
    a. Julius Caesar's spirit
    b. Calpurnia
    c. the soothsayer
    d. Cinna the Poet

Name_____

*Julius Caesar*
Final Exam—Objective Questions
page 6

47. Portia killed herself by
    a. falling on her sword
    b. swallowing fire
    c. strangling herself
    d. drowning in the Tiber

48. One element of the supernatural is apparent in the appearance of Caesar's ghost. The ghost is important because
    a. Cassius and Brutus are afraid of ghosts.
    b. it gives Antony the courage to win.
    c. it shows Caesar is the tragic hero.
    d. it shows that Caesar's spirit lives on.

49. The important military decision which Brutus makes in Act IV is to
    a. march his army to Philippi to meet Antony's army
    b. take over complete command
    c. retreat
    d. wait at Sardis for Octavius

50. A theme of this play is
    a. the downfall of an idealist in a realistic world
    b. an evil action, though nobly motivated, leads to disaster
    c. bloodshed leads to further bloodshed
    d. all of the above

51. The peak of Brutus' power is found in which scene?
    a. in the garden with Portia
    b. on the battlefield
    c. after giving Caesar's funeral oration
    d. on the street with Cassius

52. Who is the tragic hero in the play?
    a. Brutus
    b. Caesar
    c. Cassius
    d. Antony
    e. a and b

53. Shakespeare depicts characters as human beings who have varying personalities, not as stereotypes. This is shown in his characterization of Brutus, who
    a. loves Portia but is unfaithful
    b. loves Caesar as a friend but fears his power
    c. loves Cassius like a brother, but thinks he is too lean
    d. hates Portia but cries after her death

54. Antony's greed over Caesar's will, his treatment of Lepidus, and his tribute to Brutus at the end of the play illustrate Shakespeare's genius in
    a. imagery
    b. blank verse
    c. universality
    d. developing well-rounded characters

Name_____

Julius Caesar
Final Exam—Objective Questions
page 7

55. Antony's words after the assassination, "Now whilst your purpled hands do reek and smoke," illustrate that Shakespeare had great verbal facility in
    a. punning
    b. graphic description or imagery
    c. simile
    d. swearing

56. Caesar's words, "Good friends, go in and taste some wine with me" and "Caesar doth not wrong," show both his warmth and his arrogance and illustrate Shakespeare's ability to
    a. create images
    b. create puns
    c. develop characters
    d. be persuasive

57. Because the reader or theatre-goer can comprehend the reasons Shakespeare's characters act as they do, and because the themes illustrated in the play have relevance to men everywhere in all ages, Shakespeare's _____ has led to his critical acclaim.
    a. dishonesty
    b. alliteration
    c. universality
    d. political persuasion

58. Titinius was captured by the enemy army.
    a. true
    b. false

59. We never see Calpurnia's reaction to Caesar's death.
    a. true
    b. false

**Structural Terms.** Match the play event with the appropriate structural term. Some letters are used more than once.

    a. Exposition    b. Rising Action
    c. Climax    d. Falling Action    e. Resolution

_____ 60. The new triumvirate makes its plans.
_____ 61. Brutus' moral soliloquy (in his orchard)
_____ 62. Battle at Philippi
_____ 63. Flavius and Marullus scold commoners.
_____ 64. Brutus' and Antony's funeral orations
_____ 65. Caesar's ghost appears to Brutus.
_____ 66. Portia and Calpurnia warn their husbands.
_____ 67. The victors of the battle find Brutus dead and speak.
_____ 68. Brutus gets a note from "a concerned citizen."

Name_____

*Julius Caesar*
Final Exam—Objective Questions
page 8

**Indicate the SPEAKER of the following lines.**

69. "There is no terror, Cassius, in your threats/ For I am armed so strong in honesty/ That they pass by me…"
    a. Antony    b. Cassius    c. Brutus    d. Pindarus

70. "This was the noblest Roman of them all."
    a. Trebonius    b. Antony    c. Octavius    d. Cassius

71. "Beware the ides of March."
    a. Artemidorus    b. soothsayer    c. Cassius    d. Lucius

72. "The fault, dear Brutus, is not in our stars,/ But in ourselves that we are underlings."
    a. Casca    b. Antony    c. Cassius    d. Cicero

73. "Cowards die many times before their deaths.
    The valiant never taste of death but once."
    a. Octavius    b. Calpurnia    c. Cassius    d. Caesar

74. "When beggars die, there are no comets seen;
    The heavens themselves blaze forth the death of princes."
    a. Calpurnia    b. Octavius    c. Caesar    d. Portia

75. "Et tu, Brute?"
    a. Decius    b. Portia    c. Caesar    d. Antony

**Indicate the character DESCRIBED in the following lines:**

76. "Why, man, he doth bestride the narrow world/ Like a Colossus…"
    a. Caesar    b. Cassius    c. Brutus    d. Antony

77. "Yond _____ has a lean and hungry look;
    He thinks too much; such men are dangerous."
    a. soothsayer    b. Casca    c. Artemidorus    d. Cassius

78. "My heart is in the coffin there with Caesar,
    And I must pause till it come back to me."
    a. Brutus    b. Antony    c. Casca    d. Cassius

79. "Poor man! I know he would not be a wolf
    But that he sees the Romans are but sheep."
    a. Brutus    b. Cicero    c. Caesar    d. Cassius

80. "But I am as constant as the Northern star."
    a. Brutus    b. Portia    c. Cassius    d. Caesar

© Novel Units, Inc.                                All rights reserved

Name_____

*Julius Caesar*
Final Exam—Objective Questions
page 9

**Vocabulary.** Choose the definition that BEST fits the underlined word in the sentence.

81. "Thoughts of great value, worthy cogitations."
    a. meditations   b. agitations   c. reconciliations   d. mutations

82. "Alas, thou hast misconstrued everything."
    a. seen   b. misunderstood   c. figured out   d. mistreated

83. "How covert matters may be best disclosed."
    a. important   b. clearly   c. secret, hidden   d. vital

84. "Shall Rome, etc. Speak, strike, redress."
    a. get dressed   b. think   c. kill   d. set right, remedy

85. "What watchful cares do interpose themselves…
    a. disturb   b. ally   c. come between   d. throw in

86. "For I believe they are portentous things…"
    a. cloudy   b. ominous   c. thrilling   d. valuable

87. "I turn the trouble of my countenance merely upon myself…"
    a. home life   b. body   c. occupation   d. face

88. "Plucking the entrails of an offering forth…"
    a. eyebrows   b. innards   c. feathers   d. teeth

89. "But hollow men, like horses hot at hand,
    Make gallant show and promise of their mettle…"
    a. courage   b. medals   c. finances   d. foodstuff

90. "How ill this taper burns!"
    a. home   b. match   c. candle   d. firecracker

91. "Or else the world, too saucy with the gods…"
    a. charitable   b. friendly   c. clear   d. impudent

Name_____

*Julius Caesar*
Final Exam—Objective Questions
page 10

92. "Let me not hinder, Cassius, your desires..."
    a. prevent     b. add to     c. reconcile     d. cloud

93. "...he plucked me ope his doublet and offered them his throat to cut."
    a. closet     b. cupboard     c. jacket     d. sleeve

94. "...most mighty and most puissant Caesar..."
    a. humble     b. honorable     c. powerful     d. sinful

95. "Romans, countrymen, and lovers, hear me for my cause..."
    a. adulterers     b. steady dates     c. friends     d. relatives

96. "Whose ransoms did the general coffers fill..."
    a. cemeteries     b. libraries     c. parks     d. treasuries

97. "Our Caesar's vesture wounded? Look you here..."
    a. chest     b. clothing     c. stomach     d. feelings

98. "Hence! Wilt thou lift up Olympus?"
    a. athletic event  b. home of the gods  c. member of the triumvirate

99. "These couchings and these lowly courtesies..."
    a. bowings     b. sofas     c. jokes     d. threats

100. "My credit now stands on such slippery ground..."
    a. borrowing power  b. charge account  c. reputation  d. safety

© Novel Units, Inc.                                           All rights reserved

# Answer Key

**Prereading Activity #1**
190 B.C., consuls, patricians, plebeians, plunder, tribute, bribes, popular assemblies, small farmers, Rome, (Caesar, Crassus, Pompey), 60, Crassus, Caesar, Pompey, 48, Brutus, Cassius, Caesar, Octavius Caesar, Mark Antony, Lepidus, avenge Caesar's death

**Drama Terms—Prereading Activity #3**
1. subdivision of a play
2. a play that ends happily
3. conversation between characters
4. a play that ends unhappily
5. a play designed to arouse intense emotion by exaggeration and fast-moving action
6. hero or leading character with whom the audience identifies
7. person who opposes the protagonist's wishes
8. central unifying idea
9. highest point of action
10. main story
11. left of stage from actor's point of view
12. right of stage from actor's point of view
13. series of events leading to the climax
14. series of events following the climax
15. introductory section that explains the situation
16. turning point

**Drama Terms Quiz**
1. H  2. N  3. I  4. O  5. L  6. E  7. F  8. J  9. C  10. G

**Study Questions**

**Introduction**
1. He defeated Pompey.   2. 44 B.C.

**Act I**
*Scene i*
1. rule by three supposedly-equal leaders
2. The commoners are taking an undeclared holiday in honor of Caesar. The garlands on the statues are part of the celebration. This scene lets us know that not everyone in Rome is in favor of Caesar.

*Scene ii*
1. This will supposedly make her fertile.
2. Cassius, who feels Caesar has too much power, hopes to get Brutus, whom Caesar trusts, to join in the conspiracy against him.
3. He feels "lean and hungry men," like Cassius, are dangerous.
4. They want Caesar to accept the crown.
5. "The falling-down sickness"—probably epilepsy.
6. An appeal to his ego will win him over. Brutus must be convinced that the people prefer him to Caesar and that he would actually be a better leader for Rome.

*Scene iii*
1. evening
2. a slave's flaming but unharmed hand, a lion at the Capitol, an owl hooting at noon
3. Cinna and Casca have now joined.

**Act II**
*Scene i*
1. If Caesar gains too much power, he is likely to abuse it.
2. Brutus felt no oaths should be necessary among honorable Romans.
3. Brutus fears he will not go along exactly with the others' plans.

4. He thinks the citizens would consider them butchers if they kill Antony. There is no reason for it, whereas Caesar's death can be justified because he is "too ambitious" to be good for Rome.
5. He will flatter him.
6. She inflicted a wound in her thigh; he says he will tell her later.

*Scene ii*
1. a dream of Romans bathing in Caesar's blood
2. no
3. Decius explains away the dream as a good omen.

*Scene iii*
1. Send a warning letter to Caesar.

*Scene iv*
1. She is afraid of what is happening at the Capitol.

**Act III**

*Scene i*
1. "Beware the ides of March" and Artemidorus' letter.
2. (a) Metellus Cimber asked Caesar to pardon his brother. (b) Casca was the first to stab Caesar. (c) Trebonius kept an eye on Marc Antony.
3. kneels before him
4. He is not willing to go back on his word; he despises weakness.
5. He is astonished that his friend, Brutus, has betrayed him. He trusted Brutus.
6. The citizens begin rioting, "as if it is doomsday."
7. No. Lines 224-275 tell how he really feels. ("O pardon me...")
8. Octavius Caesar, Caesar's grand-nephew; Antony advises him not to come to Rome yet.

*Scene ii*
1. emotions
2. He was too ambitious.
3. "honor"—He was trying to appeal to their sense of justice and make them realize that treason is not "honorable."
4. He lets them draw their own conclusions, appeals to their reasoning faculties.
5. After Brutus' speech, they are ready to crown him. After Antony's, they want revenge for Caesar's death. The crowd is easily swayed.
6. He whets their curiosity by alluding to Caesar's will.

*Scene iii*
1. It shows the people are acting irrationally. Mob rule has taken over.

**Act IV**

*Scene i*
1. Marc Antony, Octavius, Lepidus
2. planning to kill those who conspired against Caesar
3. He is inexperienced, fit only to be an errand boy.

*Scene ii*
1. in front of Brutus' tent, in a camp near Sardis
2. They are arguing with one another.

*Scene iii*
1. Brutus refused to drop bribery charges against Lucius Pella, which Cassius requested.
2. Cassius offers to let Brutus kill him. They make peace.
3. She has committed suicide.
4. The attacking soldiers will be tired after marching so far, and will have less energy for fighting, while the troops of Brutus and Cassius will be rested.
5. He fears the troops of Octavius and Antony will pick up in numbers if they march to Sardis, since there are many citizens who want to avenge Caesar's death.
6. Cassius gives in to Brutus' wishes; they follow his plan. Cassius has taken a second seat to Brutus.

7. He says he may need them to take a message to Cassius, but perhaps he wants extra men around him as guards.
8. He tells Lucius, "If I do live I will be good to thee."
9. Caesar's ghost. "Thou shalt see me at Philippi."

**Act V**
*Scene i*
1. The plains of Philippi—where Caesar's ghost told Brutus they'd meet.
2. "But this same day must end that work the ides of March begun."
3. He is disturbed by the omens, and has some fear about losing the battle. "Their shadows seem a canopy most fatal…"
4. kill himself, rather than be taken back to Rome by Antony

*Scene ii*
1. He thought he saw Octavius' troops moving in.

*Scene iii*
1. He mistakenly reports that Titinius was taken by enemy troops.
2. He tells Pindarus to kill him "with this good sword that ran through Caesar's bowels."
3. Brutus' troops
4. Although Caesar is dead, it is because of him that the battle is fought, and lost.

*Scene iv*
1. Lucilius says he is Brutus, and is willing to die in his place.

*Scene v*
1. Dardanius, Clitus, Strato, and Volumnius stay with Brutus even though it would probably be best for them to flee.
2. that his men were all true to him
3. He is more willing to die than he was to kill Caesar.
4. He praises Brutus and says he is the only conspirator who honestly thought Caesar's death was the best thing for Rome.
5. There is optimism for Rome's future.

**Vocabulary Quiz 1**
1. concave
2. countenance
3. lamented
4. portentous
5. doublet
6. cogitations
7. plague
8. hinder
9. construe

**Vocabulary Quiz 3**
1. provender
2. covert
3. mettle
4. vaunting
5. disconsolate
6. misconstrued
7. rived

**Act I Quiz**
1. soothsayer
2. men on fire; owl hooting at noon; lion at the Capitol (any two)
3. Caesar's murder
4. If touched by a racer, she would become fertile.
5. e
6. d
7. a
8. c
9. f
10. g
11. Brutus—Cassius
12. Caesar—Mark Antony

**Act II Quiz**
1. papers he found by the window
2. his decision whether or not to join the conspiracy
3. her dream, lions born in the street, walking dead, warriors in the sky
4. Mark Antony
5. Lucius
6. Decius
7. Brutus
8. Portia
9. Artemidorus
10. Brutus, Cassius, Casca, Trebonius, Ligarius, Decius, Metellus, Cinna (any four)
11. Caesar. He would rather face life or death bravely than suffer the fear of a coward.
12. Brutus. He is comparing what Caesar might become to the emergence of a serpent.

## Act III Quiz
1. escorted Antony away from Caesar
2. Casca; Brutus
3. He is loyal to Caesar.
Essay answers will vary.

4. F
5. D
6. G

7. A
8. G
9. A

10. B
11. E
12. C

## Act IV Quiz
1. Antony, Lepidus, Octavius
2. taking bribes
3. Caesar's ghost tells him he'll see him at Philippi
4. Portia has committed suicide.
5. Cassius. He and Brutus are quarreling. Friends should see the positive, not the negative.
6. Antony. He and Octavius are discussing Lepidus. He thinks Lepidus is not good enough to be in the triumvirate.
7. Brutus. He has just seen Caesar's ghost. He is trying to tell himself his eyes are playing tricks on him.

## Act V Quiz
1. Told Cassius that Titinius was taken by the enemy.
2. Birds of prey and scavengers were following the army.
3. Asked Pindarus to stab him
4. He had Strato hold his sword, and ran on it.
5. B
6. E
7. G
8. F
9. A
10. C
11. D
12. Brutus
13. Cassius
14. Mark Antony

## Act I Activity
Rhyme scene of first poem is ABAB. Both are written in iambic pentameter. The lines from the play do not rhyme.

## Review Activity #1
1. H
2. B
3. E
4. D
5. A
6. J
7. I
8. C
9. G
10. F

## Review Activity #2
1. 7
2. 4
3. 6
4. 1
5. 8
6. 5
7. 14
8. 11
9. 2
10. 13
11. 9
12. 15
13. 10
14. 12
15. 3
16. 16

## Final Exam (Objective)

| | | | | | | | | | |
|---|---|---|---|---|---|---|---|---|---|
| 1. d | 11. a | 21. ce | 31. b | 41. c | 51. c | 61. b | 71. b | 81. a | 91. d |
| 2. d | 12. b | 22. c | 32. d | 42. c | 52. a | 62. d | 72. c | 82. b | 92. a |
| 3. e | 13. d | 23. be | 33. b | 43. c | 53. b | 63. a | 73. d | 83. c | 93. c |
| 4. c | 14. a | 24. ae | 34. d | 44. a | 54. d | 64. c | 74. a | 84. d | 94. c |
| 5. c | 15. ab | 25. b | 35. a | 45. b | 55. b | 65. d | 75. c | 85. c | 95. c |
| 6. d | 16. a | 26. b | 36. b | 46. a | 56. c | 66. b | 76. a | 86. b | 96. d |
| 7. d | 17. bc | 27. b | 37. b | 47. c | 57. c | 67. e | 77. d | 87. d | 97. b |
| 8. b | 18. d | 28. c | 38. c | 48. d | 58. b | 68. b | 78. b | 88. b | 98. b |
| 9. a | 19. bd | 29. b | 39. c | 49. a | 59. a | 69. c | 79. c | 89. a | 99. a |
| 10. c | 20. e | 30. b | 40. c | 50. d | 60. d | 70. b | 80. d | 90. c | 100. c |

© Novel Units, Inc.